A Bible Study by
Barbara L. Roose

Beautiful
Already

LEADER GUIDE

Jenny Youngman, Contributor

Reclaiming God's Perspective on Beauty

ABINGDON PRESS / NASHVILLE

BEAUTIFUL ALREADY
Reclaiming God's Perspective on Beauty
Leader Guide

Copyright © 2016 Abingdon Press
All rights reserved.

This book is printed on elemental chlorine-free paper.
ISBN 978-1-5018-1356-6

16 17 18 19 20 21 22 23 24 25—10 9 8 7 6 5 4 3 2 1
MANUFACTURED IN THE UNITED STATES OF AMERICA

Contents

About the Author

Barbara L. Roose is a popular speaker and author who is passionate about connecting women to one another and to God, helping them apply the truths of God's Word to the practical realities and challenges they face as women in today's culture. Previously Barb was Executive Director of Ministry at CedarCreek Church in Perrysburg, Ohio, where she served on staff for fourteen years and co-led the annual Fabulous Women's Conference that reached more than 10,000 women over five years. In addition to continuing as a member of the CedarCreek teaching team, Barb is a frequent speaker at women's conferences and other events. God has shaped her heart to reach out to women who either do not know or have forgotten that they are beautiful because God created them. Her desire is for every woman to realize that she has a God-given purpose and that nothing she sees in the mirror should hold her back from fulfilling that purpose. She lives in Toledo, Ohio, with her husband, Matt. They are the proud parents of three beautiful daughters, two dogs, and a grumpy rabbit named Pal.

Follow Barbara:

Twitter	@barbroose
Facebook	Facebook.com/shapestylesoul
Instagram	@barbroose
Blog	BarbRoose.com (check here for event dates and booking information)

Introduction

"I'm so fat." "I don't like my nose." "I wish I was taller." Our dissatisfaction with what we see in the mirror is what I call our ugly struggle with beauty. It's a struggle that negatively affects not only our self-image and self-esteem but also our relationships with God and others. What is the answer? We desperately need to regain God's perspective on beauty.

During this six-week Bible study, you and the women in your group will unpack the beliefs or experiences that are holding you hostage. Together you will explore God's truth about beauty throughout the Scriptures, digging into passages in both the Old and New Testaments and applying the truths in your lives. You will move away from over-focusing on unrealistic expectations and perceived flaws toward God's viewpoint of your hearts, minds, bodies, and souls. As you make this journey, you will:

- be set free from the trap of comparison and self-ridicule,
- become comfortable in your own skin, and
- reach beyond yourselves to encourage and support one another.

By learning to see the goodness, blessing, and purpose for your bodies no matter your size, shape, or style, you will overcome discontent and comparison and learn to live fully as the beautifully unique creations God designed you to be.

About the Participant Book

Before the first session, you will want to distribute copies of the participant book to the members of your group. Be sure to communicate that they are to complete the first week of readings *before* your first group session. For each week there is a main theme, a Scripture memory verse, and five readings or lessons that combine study of Scripture with personal reflection and application (**pink boldface type** indicates write-in-the-book questions and activities). Each lesson ends with two Live It Out application questions and a Talk with God prayer suggestion.

On average you will need about twenty to thirty minutes to complete each lesson. Completing these readings each week will prepare the women for the discussion and activities of the group session.

About This Leader Guide

As you gather each week with the members of your group, you will have the opportunity to watch a video, discuss and respond to what you're learning, and pray together. You will need access to a television and DVD player with working remotes.

Creating a warm and inviting atmosphere will help to make the women feel welcome. Although optional, you might consider providing snacks for your first meeting and inviting group members to rotate in bringing refreshments each week.

This leader guide and the DVD will be your primary tools for leading each group session. In this book you will find outlines for six group sessions, each formatted for either a 60-minute or 90-minute group session:

60-Minute Format
Leader Prep (Before the Session)
Preparing Your Hearts and Minds . . . . 2 minutes
Getting to Know Each Other . . . . 3–5 minutes
Video . . . . 25–30 minutes
Group Discussion . . . . 20 minutes
Closing Prayer . . . . 3 minutes

90-Minute Format
Leader Prep (Before the Session)
Preparing Your Hearts and Minds . . . . 2 minutes
Getting to Know Each Other . . . . 3–5 minutes

Video . . . . .25–30 minutes
Group Discussion . . . . .25 minutes
*Live It Out . . . . .10 minutes
*Group Activity. . . . . .15 minutes
Closing Prayer. . . . . .3 minutes

As you can see, the 90-minute format is identical to the 60-minute format but has a slightly longer discussion time plus two additional segments, which are marked above with asterisks. Feel free to adapt or modify either of these formats, as well as the individual segments and activities, in any way to meet the specific needs and preferences of your group.

Here is a brief overview of the elements included in both formats:

Leader Prep (Before the Session)

For your preparation prior to the group session, this section provides an overview of the week's Scriptures and themes, a recap of the weekly readings, a list of materials and equipment needed, and a session objective. Be sure to read this section, as well as the session outline, before the group session. If you choose, you also may find it helpful to review the DVD segment in advance.

Preparing Your Hearts and Minds (2 minutes)

You may find that participants are rushed and distracted as they arrive at Bible study (yourself included). You've had to pull away from your busy lives, schedules, and families to get there. Playing a quiet, meaningful song as everyone gathers will allow you to disconnect from the outside world and center your hearts on God. Bring an iPod or MP3 player with speakers or a CD player and CD. After the song has ended, pray either the opening prayer that is provided or one of your own.

Getting to Know Each Other (3–5 minutes)

After preparing your hearts and minds with music and prayer, use the get-to-know-you activity to engage the women in the topic while helping them to feel comfortable with one another.

Video (about 25–30 minutes)

Next, watch the week's video segment together. Be sure to direct participants to the Video Viewer Guide in the participant book, which they may complete as they watch the video.

Group Discussion (20–25 minutes depending on session length)

After watching the video, use the discussion points and questions provided to help you facilitate group discussion. You may choose to read aloud the discussion points or express them in your own words; then use one or more of the questions that follow to guide your conversation.

Note that more discussion points and questions have been provided than you will have time to include. Before the session, select those you want to cover, and put a check mark beside them. Reflect on each question and make some notes in the margins to share during your discussion time. Page references are provided for those questions that relate to specific questions or activities in the participant book. For these questions, invite group members to turn in their participant books to the pages indicated.

Depending on the number of women in your group and the level of their participation, you may not have time to cover everything you have selected, and that is OK. Rather than attempting to bulldoze through, follow the Spirit's lead and be open to where He takes the conversation. Remember that your role is not to have all of the answers but to encourage discussion and sharing.

*Live It Out (10 minutes)

If your group is meeting for 90 minutes, invite each woman to turn to a neighbor and discuss one or more challenges from the Live It Out section of the weekly readings. This will encourage the women to apply what they are learning to their daily lives as well as provide some accountability. If possible, try to come back together as a full group for the last few minutes of this segment and have participants share their responses to one of the questions.

*Group Activity (15 minutes)

If your group is meeting for 90 minutes, move next to the group activity, which involves participants in hands-on learning. Be sure to collect any necessary items in advance of the session.

Closing Prayer (3 minutes)

Close by leading the group in prayer. Invite the women to briefly name prayer requests. To get things started, you might share a personal request of your own. As women share their requests, model for the group by writing each request in your participant book, indicating that you will remember to pray for them during the week.

As the study progresses, encourage members to participate in the closing prayer by praying out loud for one another and the requests given. Ask the women to volunteer to pray for specific requests, or have each woman pray for the woman on her right or left. Make sure nametags are visible so that group members do not feel awkward if they do not remember someone's name.

After the prayer, remind the women to pray for one another throughout the week.

Before You Begin

As group leader, your role is to guide and encourage the women on the journey to see the goodness, blessing, and purpose for our bodies. The goal of the study is to equip each of you to "win" in the struggle against discontent and comparison and in your relationships with God and others. You will know that you are well on your way to victory when you no longer criticize your size, shape, or style, and become an encourager or mentor to other women, pointing them toward victory over their own ugly struggle with beauty. May God help you to create a supportive community of women as you make this powerful journey together. Remember that God will be with you every step of the way!

Leader Helps

Preparing for the Sessions

- Decide whether you will use the 60-minute or 90-minute format option. Be sure to communicate dates and times to participants in advance.
- Distribute participant books to all members at least one week before your first session and instruct them to complete the first week's readings. If you have the phone numbers or e-mail addresses of your group members, send out a reminder and a welcome.
- Check out your meeting space before each group session. Make sure the room is ready. Do you have enough chairs? Do you have the equipment and supplies you need? (See the list of materials needed in each group session outline.)
- Pray for your group and each group member by name. Ask God to work in the life of every woman in your group.
- Read and complete the week's readings in the participant book and review the session outline in the leader guide. Select the discussion points and questions you want to cover and make some notes in the margins to share in your discussion time.

Leading the Sessions

- Personally welcome and greet each woman as she arrives.
- At the start of each session, ask the women to turn off or silence their cell phones.

- Always start on time. Honor the time of those who are on time.
- Encourage everyone to participate fully, but don't put anyone on the spot. Invite the women to share as they are comfortable. Be prepared to offer a personal example or answer if no one else responds at first.
- Communicate the importance of completing the weekly readings and participating in group discussion.
- Facilitate but don't dominate. Remember that if you talk most of the time, group members may tend to listen rather than to engage. Your task is to encourage conversation and keep the discussion moving.
- If someone monopolizes the conversation, kindly thank her for sharing and ask if anyone else has any insights.
- Try not to interrupt, judge, or minimize anyone's comments or input.
- Remember that you are not expected to be the expert or have all the answers. Acknowledge that all of you are on this journey together, with the Holy Spirit as your leader and guide. If issues or questions arise that you don't feel equipped to handle or answer, talk with the pastor or a staff member at your church.
- Don't rush to fill the silence. If no one speaks right away, it's okay to wait for someone to answer. After a moment, ask, "Would anyone be willing to share?" If no one responds, try asking the question again in a different way—or offer a brief response and ask if anyone has anything to add.
- Encourage good discussion, but don't be timid about calling time on a particular question and moving ahead. Part of your responsibility is to keep the group on track. If you decide to spend extra time on a given question or activity, consider skipping or spending less time on another questions or activity in order to stay on schedule.
- Try to end on time. If you are running over, give members the opportunity to leave if they need to. Then wrap up as quickly as you can.
- Thank the women for coming and let them know you're looking forward to seeing them next time.
- Be prepared for some women to want to hang out and talk at the end. If you need everyone to leave by a certain time, communicate this at the beginning of the group session. If you are meeting in a church during regularly scheduled activities, be aware of nursery closing times.

Week 1

ALL ABOARD THE STRUGGLE BUS

Leader Prep

Scripture and Theme Overview

This week's theme is our collective struggle with shame when it comes to beauty and the way that God's truth frees us. We looked at the story of Adam and Eve in Genesis and discovered at what point shame was introduced in the human story. We also looked at the story of Rahab to discover the ways in which our beauty narratives shape us. Then we were reminded in John 8:32 that the truth about who we are and who God is will set us free from any residual shame. We also looked at the story of Rachel and Leah to explore the ways in which comparison and competition poison relationships. Finally, we reviewed the armor of God in Ephesians 6 as tools to guard our hearts.

Weekly Readings Recap

Review the key themes of the week:

Day 1: As we learn to let go of shame, judgment, and comparison and reclaim God's divine perspective on beauty, we will begin to live fully as the unique creations God designed us to be.

Day 2: Whatever your beauty narrative may be, God has created a new narrative for you—a story line in which you are treasured and valued for who He has created you to be.

Day 3: Truth sets us free from the lies we have believed about ourselves. Because God created us, loves us, and sent Jesus to deliver us and bring us a rich and satisfying life, we can trust God's truth to lead us out of the Land of Shame toward everlasting freedom.

Day 4: Comparisons divide us and can lead to a competition where there are no winners. We win when we choose to compliment rather than compete.

Day 5: Our ugly struggle with beauty impacts our hearts, making us vulnerable in those places of sensitivity. We must learn to protect our hearts and fight back with God's truth.

What You Will Need

- iPod or MP3 player with speakers or CD player and CD (see Preparing Your Hearts and Minds)
- *Beautiful Already* DVD and DVD player
- stick-on name tags and markers
- index cards and pens

Session Objective

Today you will help the women in your group let go of the shame they carry around and discover that they are beautiful because God created them.

Session Outline

Preparing Your Hearts and Minds (2 minutes)

To help the women disconnect from the outside world and center their hearts on God, play a quiet, meaningful song as the women are gathering. When you are ready to begin the session, pray the opening prayer on the next page or a prayer of your own.

Dear God,
You made us beautiful and yet we see only our flaws and feel shame. Help us to see
ourselves as You see us—lovely and fully loved. Reveal Your word to us today. Amen.

Getting to Know Each Other (3–5 minutes)

Hand out the name tags and markers, and ask participants to write their names and wear the name tags for the session. Then, ask each woman to find a partner. Ask the pairs to discuss the following questions:

- What is your go-to beauty product and why?
- When you feel your absolute best, what item from your closet are you wearing?

After a couple of minutes, come back together as a full group and have each pair quickly introduce each other to the group by their names and share something they learned about each other.

Video (25–30 minutes)

Play the Week 1 video segment on the DVD. Invite participants to complete the Video Viewer Guide for Week 1 in the participant book as they watch (page 41).

Group Discussion (20–25 minutes)

Video Discussion Questions
- How does the story of Eve shed light on our ugly struggle with beauty?
- In what ways do you struggle with shame—feeling that there is something wrong with you or that you are not enough?
- What stood out or resonated most for you from the video teaching?

Participant Book Discussion Questions

More discussion points and questions have been provided than you will have time to include. Before the session, select those you want to cover, and put a check mark beside them. Page references are provided for questions related to questions or activities in the participant book. For these questions, invite participants to share the answers they wrote in their books.

1. The phrase "ugly struggle with beauty" refers to our beauty-related challenges. This struggle is captured by our sighs and moans in front of the mirror when we look at ourselves and don't feel that we are good enough

as we are. At first, Eve didn't experience that kind of struggle. For her, there were no sighs, moans, or groans—only peace and contentment. (Day 1)

- Can you imagine standing in front of a mirror and not wishing for a little change here or there? What must that have been like for Eve?
- Do you find it easier to point out the beauty in your girlfriends than in yourself? Why do you think that is?

2. When God created humanity, He wove diversity and uniqueness into our DNA. God could have created everyone the same. He could have given us the same height, weight, shape, eye color, skin color, personality, and temperament. But He didn't. God wove diversity into our physical DNA; and as a result, we're all different colors, sizes, and shapes. Uniqueness was God's gift to us. You are unique. There is no one else like you. Uniqueness is God's gift to you. (Day 1)
   - If we were made to be unique, why do you think we try so hard to compare our beauty to the beauty of others?
   - What attributes do you have that make you unique? How difficult is it for you to accept your unique attributes as God's gift to you? Why do you think that is?
   - Read 1 Samuel 16:7 aloud. What did God tell Samuel about how we judge outward appearance versus how God judges us? What are some of the ways that you've been judged by your appearance? (pages 13–14)
   - Why is it important to remember that our beauty is given by God—and that God looks past our appearance into our hearts?

3. Your beauty narrative has been shaped by events throughout your lifetime, even those that are happening now! Most of our beauty narratives, particularly the painful ones, remain hidden in our hearts and minds until we have a safe place to share those stories. Yet when we acknowledge our narratives and place them before God, He gives us a new story line. No matter the early chapters of your life story, God's narrative for your life includes beauty and purpose. (Day 2)
   - What beauty narrative has defined you? Long-legged? Glasses? Too skinny? Too fat?
   - What is your given name? What does it mean? What was the meaning of your name as shown on UrbanDictionary.com? (page 17)
   - Read Joshua 2:1 aloud. What ideas and opinions about who Rahab is and what she values come to mind? Describe the kind of life, behaviors, or social standing that Rahab the prostitute might have experienced. (page 18)

4. While Rahab the prostitute might have been scorned and ridiculed because of what she did, there was so much more to her than just her name or label. (Day 2)
   - Read Joshua 2:8-11. What do we learn about Rahab the prostitute in these verses? (page 19)
   - In verse 11, what was Rahab's declaration regarding what she believed about God? (page 20)
   - Review Day 2. How did God shift Rahab's narrative in a new direction?

5. As women we love to heap criticism on ourselves. If someone says something negative about our size, shape, or style, we're quick to believe what they say. When we look in the mirror and focus on our flaws, we add to the negative parts of our beauty narratives. (Day 3)
   - Why do you think it is so easy to get stuck in a negative narrative about our beauty?
   - What does it feel like to be stuck in shame and regret?
   - Review Day 3. Describe the shame and regret that the prodigal son might have been feeling. What realization does the young man make in Luke 15:17-19? (page 26)

6. Because God created us, loves us, and sent Jesus to deliver us and bring us a rich and satisfying life, we can trust God's truth to lead us out of the Land of Shame toward everlasting freedom. We can't leave the Land of Shame by our own power; we have to deploy the resource of God's truth in order to break free from the shame caused by our enemy's lies and win our ugly struggle with beauty. (Day 3)
   - Read John 10:10. How does Jesus describe His purpose? How does He describe Satan's purpose? (page 27)
   - Read John 8:32. According to this verse, what sets us free? What are some truths from God's Word about who God is and His plan for your life that you need to lean into as you battle to win your ugly struggle with beauty? (page 27)
   - Name some of the lies that we encounter as women when it comes to beauty. How can these lies make us captives in the Land of Shame? (page 28)
   - What is God's truth about you? (Refer to the chart on page 28.)

7. With comparison, we're always looking at other women to see how we are similar or different in our sizes, shapes, or styles. When it comes to competition, we observe other women to see how close or far they are to our personal beauty standards. (Day 4)

- What are the three ways that comparison and competition fuel our ugly struggle with beauty? (page 30) How have you known these things to be true in your own life?
- How much pressure do you feel to fit in with our culture's definition of beauty? (page 30) Where does the pressure come from?
- What is a good measure for *you* in determining how much pressure you're feeling to measure up? The amount of new beauty-related products or clothing you desire to purchase? The level of dissatisfaction with your wardrobe? Something else?

8. Christian women aren't immune to comparison or competition. There's a difference between noticing and comparing. The difference comes down to whether or not I'm looking for something to compliment or something to criticize. The weapon that overpowers competition and comparison is love. (Day 4)
   - Review Day 4. How were Leah and Rachel trapped in a relationship of competition and comparison?
   - Were you ever compared physically to another woman, either as a child or as an adult? If so, how did you feel about the comparisons? What feelings and memories still linger today? (page 34)
   - Read 1 Corinthians 13:4-7. How can these verses remind you to look at other women with love, rather than with an attitude of comparison and competition? If you begin to look at all women with love, how could that help you to look at yourself less critically? (page 35)

9. When it comes to our ugly struggle with beauty, our hearts, minds, and bodies also need protection. (Day 5)
   - Read Proverbs 4:23. Why is it imperative that we guard our hearts? (page 38)
   - Read Colossians 2:8. What are some of the ways that you see women, including yourself, being taken captive by the world's concept of beauty? The Apostle Paul refers to two influences that we can be taken captive through, becoming victims by fraud. What are these influences? (page 39)

10. We never have to feel helpless in our ugly struggle with beauty! (Day 5)
    - Read Ephesians 6:10-17. Name the weapons God gives us that we can use to win our ugly struggle with beauty. (page 40)
    - Which weapons do you need to deploy *right now* in your ugly struggle with beauty? (page 40)
    - Review your "attack plan." (pages 39–40) How will you take action against your ugly struggle with beauty from here on?

11. Wrap up group discussion with these questions:
    - What is something that surprised you in your study this week?
    - What did you learn this week about God? About yourself?
    - How does it impact your life to realize that you can be free from the ugly struggle with beauty?

*Live It Out Discussion (10 minutes)

If you are meeting for 90 minutes, ask everyone to turn to a neighbor and talk about one or more of the **Live It Out** reflections from the weekly readings. If possible, try to come back together for the last few minutes of this segment and invite a few volunteers to share some highlights from their conversations.

*Group Activity (15 minutes)

Give everyone two index cards and a pen. On the first card, have each woman write the name of the person sitting to her right. Below the name, she is to write affirming words and compliments about her neighbor. She doesn't need to know her well—only to write words of encouragement and affirmation. When all are finished writing, they can give the cards to their neighbors.

Next, invite participants to write their own name on the second card. This time they should write words of encouragement and affirmation to themselves. After a few minutes, ask:

- What was easier to write—words of affirmation to your neighbor or to yourself? Why?
- How can we train ourselves to keep a positive and encouraging narrative in our minds instead of defaulting to shame, regret, competition, or comparison?

Closing Prayer (3 minutes)

Close the session by taking personal prayer requests from group members and leading the group in prayer. As you progress to later weeks in the study, encourage members to participate in the closing prayer by praying out loud for one another and the requests given. Remind group members to pray for one another throughout the week.

Week 2

DEFINING DIVINE BEAUTY

Leader Prep

Scripture and Theme Overview

This week's theme is about understanding true beauty—divine beauty—by knowing who God is. We looked at Scriptures about holiness and descriptions of divine beauty. We searched the Scriptures to discover truths about God's character and what God thinks about beauty. We ended the week focusing on Philippians 4:8 as a tool to replace the narrative of the ugly struggle with a new narrative of good, right, lovely, and praiseworthy things.

Weekly Readings Recap

Review the key themes of the week:

Day 1: Divine beauty is the true, good, and beautiful nature of God. It is the highest form of beauty possible. In our humanity, it's impossible for us to attain the same level of beauty as God, but we can reflect His character—His divine beauty—in our lives.

Day 2: Our struggle with beauty has to do with holiness. When we look in the mirror, we should remember that we are created in God's image and that God invites us to share in His holy nature by walking in His truth, goodness, and beauty.

Day 3: Based on what we see around us, God cares about beauty. Beauty in nature reveals to us the character of God. We cannot know beauty until we know God.

Day 4: God wants us to pay attention to beauty and to recognize His power over all things, both great and small. God cares for all the details of our lives.

Day 5: When we pursue holiness in our lives, our focus shifts from conforming to transforming—from going with the crowd to moving in a new direction by allowing God to change the way we think about beauty. As we discover certain beauty myths that are untrue, God's truth integrates into our thinking and transforms our minds.

What You Will Need

- iPod or MP3 player with speakers or CD player and CD (see Preparing Your Hearts and Minds)
- *Beautiful Already* DVD and DVD player
- stick-on name tags and markers
- card stock or craft paper and markers

Session Objective

Today you will help the women in your group redefine beauty according to God's perspective.

Session Outline

Preparing Your Hearts and Minds (2 minutes)

To help the women disconnect from the outside world and center their hearts on God, play a quiet, meaningful song as the women are gathering. When you are ready to begin the session, pray the opening prayer below or a prayer of your own.

Dear God, thank You for another week of discovering Your perspective on beauty. Continue to reveal Your truth and love to us today as we open Your Word and share together. Amen.

Getting to Know Each Other (3–5 minutes)

Hand out the name tags and markers, and ask participants to write their names and wear the name tags for the session. Then ask each woman to find a partner. Ask the pairs to discuss the following questions:

- What is the most beautiful place you've ever seen on earth?
- How do you respond when someone tells you that you look beautiful?

After a couple of minutes, come back together as a full group and have each pair quickly introduce each other to the group by their names and share something they learned about each other.

Video (25–30 minutes)

Play the Week 2 video segment on the DVD. Invite participants to complete the Video Viewer Guide for Week 2 in the participant book as they watch (page 69).

Group Discussion (20–25 minutes)

Video Discussion Questions

- How does the reminder that beauty is God's creation, not ours, help you in your ugly struggle with beauty?
- Why is it important for us to recognize that beauty is a spiritual matter and to define beauty through the lens of God's nature or character?
- What stood out or resonated most for you from the video teaching?

Participant Book Discussion Questions

More discussion points and questions have been provided than you will have time to include. Before the session, select those you want to cover, and put a check mark beside them. Page references are provided for questions related to questions or activities in the participant book. For these questions, invite participants to share the answers they wrote in their books.

1. In our culture, there is no absolute definition of beauty. Scientists have tried to apply objective constructs to measure beauty. They've measured for proportionality and symmetry or harmony, but to no avail. Our best human thinking about beauty is caught up in a black hole that just absorbs our inputs and opinions but never reveals a true answer. (Day 1)
   - Why is the phrase "beauty is in the eye of the beholder" problematic?
   - How do *you* define beauty? (page 45)
   - Why should any attempt to define beauty begin with God?

2. When we know God's character, then we know more about who we are. Any attempt to explain beauty must stem from God's divine character—and nothing else—because God is the originator of beauty. This is why we call the highest form of beauty divine beauty. (Day 1)
   - What three qualities of God's character are integrally related to divine beauty?
   - Which of these three aspects or characteristics of God's divine beauty do you need to reflect more often? (page 49) Why?
   - Divine beauty is the true, good, and beautiful nature of God. How does this definition of divine beauty compare or contrast with some of the more popular cultural definitions of beauty? (page 49)

3. God is holy or set apart because His nature is the ultimate and unmatched in truth, goodness, and beauty. His nature provides a different measuring stick than our culture's standards for truth, goodness, and beauty. (Day 2)
   - What did you learn this week about the difference between God's standard of beauty and our culture's standards?
   - Do you think it is easier or more difficult to meet God's standard rather than our culture's standards? Why?
   - Read 1 Corinthians 6:19-20. Where is the temple of the Holy Spirit? According to this verse, why does God have the right to command us to live in holiness? What does it mean that we were bought with a price? How are we to respond? (page 52)

4. Most of us deeply desire to be holy and to honor God with how we "live out" beauty in our lives, but there are some areas where we struggle. If we are really being honest, there are some areas where we reject God's way in favor of our own thinking or behavior, which God calls sin. There are other areas where we are uncertain and need guidance. Some of us wonder if there is a list of dos and don'ts for Christian women when it comes to beauty. Some women want to know if God approves of Botox or cosmetic surgery. Other women want to know how much is too much to spend on a piece of clothing or how many pairs of shoes a "good Christian woman" should own. (Day 2)
   - Read 1 Corinthians 10:23. What is the attitude of the Corinthians and the response that Paul gives them? (page 53)
   - What are your thoughts about cosmetic procedures and plastic surgery? Why do you think some Christian women feel uncomfortable talking about these topics? What other beauty-related topics do you see causing confusion among Christian women? (page 54)
   - Read 1 Corinthians 10:31. What counsel do we receive from this verse? How could you apply this counsel to your clothing closet, beauty regimen,

and shopping habits? What is the attitude and purpose that must govern *all* of our beauty-related decisions? (pages 54–55)

5. Based on what we see around us, God cares about beauty. God could have created the heavens and the earth in a monotone color scheme or black and white, but He didn't. God didn't have to create flowers in breathtaking, vibrant colors, but He did. Our world could have been so different, yet God has revealed His beautiful character in the world around us. (Day 3)
   - What are some of the most beautiful things you've ever seen?
   - What do you think about God when you look at a sunset or a flower or the mountains?
   - Read Genesis 1. What phrase is repeated multiple times in this chapter to describe God's creations? (page 58) Do you find it difficult to apply that stamp of approval to yourself? Why or why not?

6. God values physical beauty and intentionally shares it with us. Beauty in nature reveals to us the character of God. We cannot know beauty until we know God. (Day 3)
   - Have you ever tried to disregard your beauty as irrelevant or insignificant? If so, why do you think you've done this?
   - Considering that God created such beauty in this world and that God created you, what do you think about the depth of your beauty now?
   - Share how you completed this statement: When I look at the world around me, I know that God values beauty because… (page 60)

7. God recognizes that we have need for clothing and must cover our bodies, yet God doesn't want us to get caught up in obsessing over what we're going to wear. This obsession relates to those who continually purchase volumes of clothes as well as those of us who stand in our closets each morning and bemoan the task of getting dressed. (Day 4)
   - Describe a time when you found yourself obsessing about your next clothing purchase or what you were going to wear. (page 62)
   - How often are you uncomfortable in your clothes or self-conscious about what you are wearing? How can we take proper care and attention with our clothes without being obsessive about it? Where should we draw the line? (page 62)
   - Read Matthew 6:25-31. What did Jesus tell the people to avoid? (page 63) When have you worried about these things?
   - Why do you think we are so prone to worry about what we're wearing?

8. In our beauty-conscious culture, conforming happens when we take our attitudes and beliefs from the world around us regarding what we should

wear, how we should pose or act, or how we should interpret what we see in the mirror. When we conform, we chase the ideas of an elusive beauty that we all want to catch and claim. Even if we are not chasing beauty, we are secretly envious of the ones who are. Maybe we aren't trying because we don't think we can do it, so we're lamenting the fact that we'll never be that kind of beauty. (Day 5)

- Have you ever struggled with envy?
- In what ways have you chased beauty?
- Read Romans 12:2. What is the evidence that we are conforming to this world? What is the key to our transformation? How does God change us into new persons? (page 65)

9. When it comes to beauty, we move from conforming to transforming by allowing God to change the way we think about beauty. There are certain beauty myths that we discover are untrue, and as God transforms our minds, His truth integrates into our thinking. (Day 5)

- Read Philippians 4:8. Share what you wrote in the blanks to indicate what God wants us to think about. (page 66) How can these things change our understanding of our beauty?
- What are some of the challenges you face when it comes to changing your thoughts about the areas where you struggle with beauty? (page 67)
- Have you noticed any changes in your thinking since beginning this study? (page 67)

10. Wrap up group discussion with these questions:

- What is something that surprised you in your study this week?
- What did you learn this week about God? About yourself?
- How does understanding divine beauty impact your life and how you see yourself?

*Live It Out (10 minutes)

If you are meeting for 90 minutes, ask everyone to turn to a neighbor and talk about one or more of the **Live It Out** reflections from the weekly readings. If possible, try to come back together for the last few minutes of this segment and invite a few volunteers to share some highlights from their conversations.

*Group Activity (15 minutes)

Hand out sheets of card stock or craft paper and markers. Ask participants to write Philippians 4:8 decoratively onto their paper. As they work, encourage them to memorize and meditate on the verse. When they are finished, ask the women to read aloud with you the fill-in-the-blank statements about this verse from Day 5 (page 66). Acknowledge that depending on the Bible translation they used, they may have written different words in the blanks. Everyone should say aloud whatever words they wrote.

Instead of lies, fix your thoughts on what's <u>true</u>.
Instead of what's dishonorable, fix your thoughts on what's <u>honorable</u>.
Instead of what's wrong, fix your thoughts on what's <u>right</u>.
Instead of lewd or impure things, fix your thoughts on what's <u>pure</u>.
Instead of ugly or trashy things, fix your thoughts on what's <u>lovely</u>.
Instead of what's despicable or unworthy, fix your thoughts on what's <u>admirable</u>.
Instead of what's inferior, fix your thoughts on what's <u>excellent</u>.
Instead of complaints, fix your thoughts on what's worthy of <u>praise</u>.

Closing Prayer (3 minutes)

Close the session by taking personal prayer requests from group members and leading the group in prayer. As you progress to later weeks in the study, encourage members to participate in the closing prayer by praying out loud for one another and the requests given. Remind group members to pray for one another throughout the week.

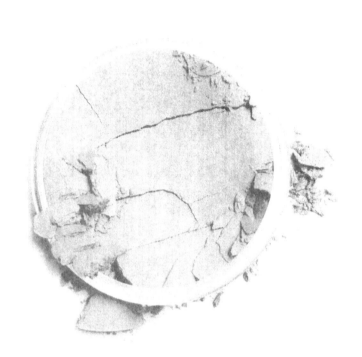

Week 3

CELEBRATING WHAT WE SEE

Leader Prep

Scripture and Theme Overview

This week's theme taught us that seeking God first can help with our perspective on what we see in the mirror each day. We dug into Scriptures about seeking God first, such as Matthew 6:33 and Romans 14:17. Then we explored the goodness, blessing, and purpose of our bodies and acknowledged that we are unique masterpieces of God (Genesis 1; Jeremiah 29:11; Psalm 139:14; Ephesians 2:10). We also looked at our differences and how we are to relate to one another, as well as scriptural support for the importance of unity (Genesis 1:27; John 13:34; Romans 10:12; 1 Corinthians 12:12-13; Ephesians 2:14-15; 1 John 2:9-11). The stories of Esther and Jacob helped us to understand what it means to be chosen by God, and passages in both the Old and New Testaments reminded us that we are enough in God's eyes—and free from condemnation.

Weekly Readings Recap

Review the key themes of the week:

Day 1: We must prioritize the "mirrors" in our lives, remembering that not all images are true images for us to believe. The only mirror that matters is God's mirror. Every time we look in the mirror is an opportunity for us to seek and connect with God, which leads to deep and abiding satisfaction.

Day 2: We are all unique creations—masterpieces of God. When we affirm the goodness, blessing, and purpose of our bodies, we reshape how we see ourselves and allow our God-given beauty to shine through.

Day 3: We cannot experience the totality of beauty if we hold onto our prejudice. There is great beauty in our unity.

Day 4: Too often we let our life circumstances convince us that God doesn't care. But even when we reject God, He still chooses us. Understanding what it means for God to choose us now and forever sets us free from feelings of inadequacy and failure.

Day 5: When we blame ourselves for behavior that we think we should be able to control, we can't love ourselves. When this happens, we start thinking that maybe God can't love us either because we have failed in some area. But God always sees us as enough, even when we make mistakes. If we are in Christ, God doesn't condemn us, no matter what the face in the mirror wants us to believe.

What You Will Need

- iPod or MP3 player with speakers or CD player and CD (see Preparing Your Hearts and Minds)
- *Beautiful Already* DVD and DVD player
- stick-on name tags and markers
- paper and pens

Session Objective

Today you will help the women in your group celebrate what they see in the mirror, replacing damaging, negative comments with the truth of how God sees us—inside and out.

Session Outline

Preparing Your Hearts and Minds (2 minutes)

To help the women disconnect from the outside world and center their hearts on God, play a quiet, meaningful song as the women are gathering. When you are ready to begin the session, pray the opening prayer below or a prayer of your own.

Dear God, when we look in the mirror, we aren't always thrilled with what we see. Give us eyes to see what You see and gratitude for all You made us to be. Reveal Your truth to us today. Amen.

Getting to Know Each Other (3–5 minutes)

Hand out the name tags and markers, and ask participants to write their names and wear the name tags for the session. Then, ask each woman to find a partner. Ask the pairs to discuss the following questions:

- What is your morning beauty routine?
- What is usually your first thought when you look in the mirror first thing in the morning?

After a couple of minutes, come back together as a full group and have each pair quickly share something they learned about each other.

Video (25–30 minutes)

Play the Week 3 video segment on the DVD. Invite participants to complete the Video Viewer Guide for Week 3 in the participant book as they watch (page 97).

Group Discussion (20–25 minutes)

Video Discussion Questions

- How can seeking God first help us in our ugly struggle with beauty?
- What does it mean to see God first when you look in the mirror? How might this practice change the way that you think and live?
- What stood out or resonated most for you from the video teaching?

Participant Book Discussion Questions

More discussion points and questions have been provided than you will have time to include. Before the session, select those you want to cover, and put a check mark beside them. Page references are provided for questions related to questions or activities in the participant book. For these questions, invite participants to share the answers they wrote in their books.

1. When we look in a physical mirror, we capture a picture of what we see. Then we assign value to what we see—good or bad. If we allow others to

act as mirrors for us, they capture a picture of what they see and then decide whether what they see is good or bad. (Day 1)

- How does the concept of a mirror relate to our beauty narratives?
- Which mirrors influence you most these days? (page 74)
- What are the positives and negatives associated with each of the three types of mirrors? (page 74)

2. Seeking the kingdom of God means that we stop searching for approval from others or even for self-affirmation. Seeking is serious business. It's more than just looking, as in looking for one's keys or an outfit to wear. In this case, seeking is a high-stakes pursuit of searching—the kind of searching a parent does when a child wanders off in the store. That's the kind of seeking that God wants us to do. We're not called to look for a casual connection with God. Rather, we're called to devote our effort and energy to connecting intimately with Him. (Day 1)

- Read Matthew 6:33. On a scale of 1 ("not really") to 10 ("whole-heartedly"), how much are you prioritizing God with regard to your heart, mind, body, and soul? (page 77)
- What are the areas in your life where you are seeking God? (page 77)
- How could seeking God first change the way we see ourselves in the mirror?

3. God wants us to shine as beacons on a hill. We are designed to radiate His truth and beauty to women in our world who are desperate to find a beauty that is pure and true. Yet our God-given beauty cannot shine through if we are covering it up with bad attitudes or beliefs about ourselves. Our God-given beauty cannot shine through if we are carrying ourselves as if we are an afterthought—as if our bodies have not been specially designed for us. (Day 2)

- If everything that God created is good, including humans, then why do we struggle to recognize God's goodness in our bodies? (page 80)
- How does struggling with our beauty keep us from shining like a beacon on a hill?
- What can we do to let go of bad attitudes and beliefs about ourselves and live into the truth that our bodies were specially designed for us?

4. Each part of the human body has a God-defined purpose. We often condemn certain features of our bodies rather than give thanks for them. We are all unique creations, and God has a specific plan and purpose for our hearts, minds, bodies, and life experiences. (Day 2)

- Read Ephesians 2:10. What role do our bodies play in God's purposes in this world? (page 82)

- How are our bodies tools for God to use?
- How is your physical body a blessing to you?

5. It is possible for us to enjoy our distinctive beauty and still find the beauty in one another whatever our skin color. (Day 3)
   - Our comfort level with the topic of race often depends on our background and life experience. When are you comfortable talking about race? When do you become uncomfortable? (page 85)
   - What was your experience with race growing up? (page 85)
   - How have your early experiences with race impacted your life as an adult? (page 85)

6. Let's be honest. We've all thought that we are better than someone else. While it doesn't always feel safe to do so, I believe that there are occasions when racial healing could occur if we would acknowledge our individual prejudice. We cannot experience the totality of beauty if we hold onto our prejudice. You and I have to challenge those pre-formed negative thoughts. (Day 3)
   - How might acknowledging and talking about prejudice help us to experience the beauty that God intended in making us each unique?
   - How can acknowledging and talking about prejudice lead to unity?
   - Read Ephesians 2:14-15. Why is unity so important? What impact could we, the church, have in our world if we were to truly love and care for everyone, no matter their race, color, or culture? (page 87)

7. Did you know that God chooses you? You look in the mirror and see your wrong choices, awful mistakes, shortcomings, or bad behavior, but God still chooses you. Even if you look in the mirror and see only a woman who has been brutally victimized by others, God still chooses you. He always has. Too often we let our life circumstances convince us that He doesn't care. But even when we reject God, He still chooses us. (Day 4)
   - What are some times when we women long to be chosen? What are some of the ugly consequences that can happen when we aren't chosen? How do we sometimes respond? (page 91)
   - What does it mean to you that God has chosen you? To what extent do you believe this is true? (page 91)
   - Read Hebrews 13:5b. What promise does God make to us? (page 91)
   - How does knowing that God chooses you change the way you see yourself?

8. Our greatest fear in life is rejection, the horrific sensation that we are not good enough to be loved. This becomes a particularly sensitive area for single women who desire to find love, companionship, and marriage.

But we all struggle with the fear of rejection at various times and in various ways. This fear is amplified when we think that rejection is our fault because of how we look. When someone is with us, that means something! Walking shoulder-to-shoulder with someone evokes confidence and the feeling that we are not alone. (Day 4)

- Read Zephaniah 3:17. What does it say that God will do? (page 91)
- How could being more connected to God alleviate your fears of loneliness or rejection? (page 91)
- How can these Scripture promises guard your heart the next time you feel passed over or dismissed?

9. As we beat ourselves up with words or thoughts or lack of self-care, we heap shame on ourselves, hoping that we will change if we feel bad enough about our behavior. Here is an important truth: shame doesn't work. Shaming yourself never creates lasting, positive results. Shame can jumpstart a behavior change, but it cannot sustain it. Shame or embarrassment can drive us to throw on the brakes, but moving forward in shame or embarrassment is painful, and we do not thrive that way. (Day 5)

- Why do you think we are so hard on ourselves?
- Now that we are halfway through our study, what have you learned about how God feels about you?
- Read Psalm 139:17-18. What does the psalmist say about how God feels about us? When you mess up, how do you think God really feels about you in that moment? (page 94)

10. Condemnation is like a heavy, leaded blanket. It wraps around our bodies and weighs us down. Are you carrying a blanket of condemnation? If so, you can toss that blanket on the ground. Where there is condemnation, there is no hope. But Jesus Christ is the hope of the world! (Day 5)

- Read Jeremiah 31:3. How hard or easy is it for you to embrace that you are loved unconditionally by God, no matter what? Why? (page 94)
- Read Lamentations 3:21-23. What do these verses tell us about God's love and mercy? (page 95)
- When you think about God's mercy being renewed each morning in your life, how can that bring you hope when you make mistakes? (page 95)

11. Even if what you are struggling with isn't your fault, you have to fight against the self-condemning thoughts that you should have been stronger or that you should have stopped what happened. Always remember this: if you are in Christ, God doesn't condemn you, no matter what the face in the mirror wants you to believe. (Day 5)

- Read Romans 8:1. What is the truth declared in this verse?

- How can this promise help you look in the mirror and love yourself more fully?
- What condemning messages do you need to let go of in order to live in the freedom and grace God intends for you?

12. Wrap up group discussion with these questions:
- What is something that surprised you in your study this week?
- What did you learn this week about God? About yourself?
- How does it impact your life to realize that God never condemns you?

*Live It Out (10 minutes)

If you are meeting for 90 minutes, ask everyone to turn to a neighbor and talk about one or more **Live It Out** reflections from the weekly readings. If possible, try to come back together for the last few minutes of this segment and invite a few volunteers to share some highlights from their conversations.

*Group Activity (15 minutes)

Hand out sheets of paper and ask participants to number the page from 1 to 20. Ask them to write twenty statements that are positive, affirming, and encouraging about their physical bodies. For example: "I have strong legs." "I like my smile." When they are finished, talk about how easy or difficult it was to find twenty positive things to write. Ask some volunteers to share something they like about themselves. Encourage them to keep this list somewhere they can find it when they need to remember the good things.

Closing Prayer (3 minutes)

Close the session by taking personal prayer requests from group members and leading the group in prayer. Invite members to participate in the closing prayer as they are willing by praying out loud for one another and the requests given. Remind group members to pray for one another throughout the week.

Week 4

GENTLE AND QUIET BEAUTY

Leader Prep

Scripture and Theme Overview

This week's theme is that true beauty flows from the inside out. We began by unpacking the specific qualities of inner beauty, which led us to Scriptures that help us understand what it means to have a gentle and quiet spirit. Then Colossians 2:7 gave us instruction about growing deep roots in our faith. We also looked to Jesus' teaching about how often we should forgive others, as well as the Apostle Paul's Letter to the Romans for promises about our freedom from condemnation. Finally, we looked to Ruth and Naomi to teach us about spiritual friendship.

Weekly Readings Recap

Review the key themes of the week:

Day 1: The unfading beauty of a gentle and quiet spirit attracts and blesses because it is others-focused rather than self-centered or inward-focused. It also is willing to yield when appropriate. When we submit to the authority of an all-knowing, all-powerful, ever-present Creator God, we possess a beautiful tranquility and peace because we don't have to worry about anything. We are confident that He will take care of us.

Day 2: We can stand tall and maintain our God-given gift of beauty in a world that wants to destroy that gift when we have strong faith roots to hold us up. The strength of our faith directly correlates to how we will manage our beauty narratives, how we will allow culture to influence our ideas about beauty, and how resilient we will be when faced with challenges or hardships.

Day 3: There is one thing guaranteed to make or keep a woman ugly: unforgiveness. Forgiveness opens our hearts and allows our beauty to shine through.

Day 4: We need friendships with other women as we battle our ugly struggle with beauty. Once we finally believe we are beautiful because God created us, we need supportive, godly women in our lives to encourage us and remind us of that truth.

Day 5: As women, we need different kinds of community in our lives because God ministers to us through different interpersonal dynamics. Three kinds of relationships that support us in winning our ugly struggle with beauty are spiritual friends, mentors, and go-to girls.

What You Will Need

- iPod or MP3 player with speakers or CD player and CD (see Preparing Your Hearts and Minds)
- *Beautiful Already* DVD and DVD player
- stick-on name tags and markers
- thank you cards and envelopes

Session Objective

Today you will help the women in your group reflect on inner beauty and discover how inner beauty radiates out and blesses others.

Session Outline

Preparing Your Hearts and Minds (2 minutes)

To help the women disconnect from the outside world and center their hearts on God, play a quiet, meaningful song as the women are gathering. When you are ready to begin the session, pray the opening prayer below or a prayer of your own.

Dear God, thank You for creating us and calling us beautiful. Help us to see ourselves as You do. Teach us what inner beauty means and how to let our beauty shine out from within and bless others. Amen.

Getting to Know Each Other (3–5 minutes)

Hand out the name tags and markers, and ask participants to write their names and wear the name tags for the session. Then, ask each woman to find a partner. Ask the pairs to discuss the following:

- Who is someone you know who radiates inner beauty? What is one quality that makes her beautiful?
- After a couple of minutes, come back together as a full group and have each pair quickly share a quality that makes someone radiate inner beauty.

Video (25–30 minutes)

Play the Week 4 video segment on the DVD. Invite participants to complete the Video Viewer Guide for Week 4 in the participant book as they watch (pages 130–131).

Group Discussion (20–25 minutes)

Video Discussion Questions

- What does a gentle and quiet spirit have to do with beauty? What new insights have you gained about what it means to have a gentle and quiet spirit?
- How can our inability to forgive affect the ability of others to see God's beauty in us?
- What stood out or resonated most for you from the video teaching?

Participant Book Discussion Questions

More discussion points and questions have been provided than you will have time to include. Before the session, select those you want to cover, and put a check mark beside them. Page references are provided for questions related to questions or activities in the participant book. For these questions, invite participants to share the answers they wrote in their books.

1. The unfading beauty of a gentle and quiet spirit attracts and blesses because this is a woman who is others-focused rather than self-centered or inward-focused. (Day 1)
   - Read 1 Peter 3:3-4. What kind of beauty did Peter want the women to cultivate?
   - Why would Peter describe the qualities of inner beauty as "unfading"? What gives them eternal staying power? (page 100)
   - How would you define a gentle and quiet spirit in your own words? (page 101)
   - Name a woman in your life who exemplifies a gentle and quiet spirit. (Perhaps recall the woman you described in the Getting to Know Each Other activity.) What can you learn from her that you can apply in your own life? (page 102)

2. Submission is about trust. When we submit, we recognize that we don't always have to be right and we don't always have to have our way. God is in charge of all of the details of our lives—over and above those of everyone else. When we show respect and deference to others, we are ultimately submitting to God. (Day 1)
   - Where are the places or relationships in your life where you may need to demonstrate submission? (page 103)
   - What feels threatening about submission? (page 104)
   - How do you think your desire to cultivate inner beauty will be impacted if you shy away from submission? (page 104)

3. If we expect to stand tall, we must have strong roots holding us up. A tree doesn't rely on other trees to prop it up; it stands or falls based on the integrity and stability of its roots. The quality and amount of fruit a tree produces depends on the strength of the foundation of the tree. The same goes for you and me. (Day 2)
   - Read Colossians 2:7. As Christians, who is our taproot? (page 107) What does this passage teach us about being deeply rooted in Christ?
   - What fruit grows from us when we have deep roots? How does this relate to our struggle with beauty?
   - What are the ABCs of our foundation of faith? What are some specific areas in your development of the ABCs that you need to address? (pages 109–110) Have the women turn to a neighbor and share briefly. Encourage them to pray for one another in the coming week.

4. The best way to cultivate trust in God is to read and memorize Scripture. It not only nourishes our roots but it's also like a GPS. Whenever I need strength or redirection, I pull GPS verses from my memory and allow God's powerful, unchanging, life-giving words to encourage and sustain my heart. (Day 2)
    - Read Ephesians 3:17. According to this verse, what do you need to do so that your roots will grow deeper in Christ? Where are the places where you need to trust God more in your life? (pages 109–110)
    - What is a GPS verse you attempted to memorize this week? What drew you to this verse? (page 111)
    - How can memorizing Scripture help us to trust God more?

5. When someone hurts our feelings or does something to us, our faces pucker and our bodies tense up. Our shoulders draw back and our fists clench. We lose the supple fluidity of our movements, our beautiful gracefulness. Unforgiveness is ugly. And my friends, God don't like ugly. (Day 3)
    - When have you felt yourself puckering up, getting tense, or tightening up because of hurt feelings?
    - Why is unforgiveness ugly?
    - What does forgiveness have to do with our ugly struggle with beauty?

6. When we don't practice forgiveness, each offense becomes like a brick wall in the heart. Brick walls can be protective, but they also can be barriers. Some of you have built barriers in your hearts. You've been hurt so much by so many people that you've built brick walls twenty feet high. (Day 3)
    - Read Matthew 18:21-22. What was Jesus' response to Peter's question? What happens to us when we keep score on the people who hurt or offend us? (page 114)
    - What are some of the ugly feelings associated with unforgiveness? (page 114)
    - Read Colossians 3:13. What does it mean to make allowances for one another's faults? How can we do this? (page 115)

7. There is a difference between knowing lots of people and being connected. Connection happens when we allow ourselves to be known and we get to know others. Some of you avoid this connection out of fear; others just don't think you need a close connection. (Day 4)
    - What difference does having a real connection make—as opposed to simply knowing lots of people? What does it feel like to have a deep connection with a friend?
    - How can deep friendships help us with our ugly struggle with beauty?

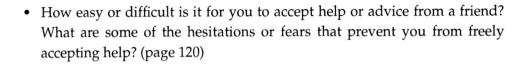

- How easy or difficult is it for you to accept help or advice from a friend? What are some of the hesitations or fears that prevent you from freely accepting help? (page 120)

8. We were not designed to be alone. The beauty of our female hearts is that they were created to love, share, nurture, and bless other women, who have lives just as complicated as our own. (Day 4)
    - Imagine that you are a porcupine. When are you more likely to put up your "quills" in conversations or interactions with other women? (page 122)
    - Read Romans 12:18. According to this verse, what is your responsibility? (page 122)
    - What can you do to deepen some of your friendships?

9. As women, we need different kinds of community in our lives because God ministers to us through different interpersonal dynamics. (Day 5)
    - What are the kinds of relationships discussed on Day 5? Describe in your own words each type of relationship.
    - Read Ecclesiastes 4:9-12. What is the danger of solitude? What are the blessings that come from partnering with others? (page 124)
    - How have you been blessed by a spiritual friendship or mentoring relationship?

10. Like Ruth and Naomi, "go-to girls" are there for each other no matter what! These friendships are characterized by vulnerability, transparency, and high levels of trust. This means that "go-to girl" relationships are scary at the beginning because trust must be built over time. (Day 5)
    - Read Ruth 1:16-18. What did Ruth declare to Naomi? (page 128)
    - Do you have any current and active "go-to girl" relationships? (page 128) If so, how have these relationships been a blessing in your life? If not, is there a special woman in your life whom you would like to become a "go-to girl"?
    - How can we develop go-to girl relationships? Which of the tips on page 128 could be helpful to you? Are there others you might add to the list?

11. Wrap up group discussion with these questions:
    - What is something that surprised you in your study this week?
    - What did you learn this week about God? About yourself?
    - How does it impact your life to realize that true beauty flows from the inside out?

*Live It Out (10 minutes)

If you are meeting for 90 minutes, ask everyone to turn to a neighbor and talk about one or more **Live It Out** reflections from the weekly readings. If possible, try to come back together for the last few minutes of this segment and invite a few volunteers to share some highlights from their conversations.

*Group Activity (15 minutes)

Hand out thank you cards and envelopes. Ask participants to think about someone who has been a spiritual friend, mentor, or go-to girl and write her a letter of gratitude for the friendship. If anyone feels she does not have these kinds of friends, she can choose a person who has been special in her life. Encourage participants to tell these persons how their inner beauty radiates outward and blesses others.

Closing Prayer (3 minutes)

Close the session by taking personal prayer requests from group members and leading the group in prayer. Encourage members to participate in the closing prayer by praying out loud for one another and the requests given. Remind group members to pray for one another throughout the week.

Week 5

WINNING OUR UGLY STRUGGLE

Leader Prep

Scripture and Theme Overview

This week's theme is that inner beauty flows out of us toward others when we experience Jesus' peace and healing. We explored how we become fragmented and broken inside when we allow others to define our identities, rather than Christ, and we searched the Scriptures for promises about our true identities in Christ. We read in Mark 5 about the hemorrhaging woman who found healing and peace through Christ's power, which is available to us as well regardless of the nature of our wounds. We were reminded that Christ came to set us free from the painful consequences of sin (Isaiah 61:1-3; John 16:33), and that His scars represent our healing from sin and shame. We also studied Scriptures that point to God's delight in aromas as well as verses that show us how our lives can be a pleasing aroma to God (Leviticus 1:9; 2:2; 23:18; Ephesians 5:2; 2 Corinthians 2:14-16). Finally, we saw that God takes care of us so that we can take care of ourselves, and we looked specifically to 1 Corinthians 6:19-20 and Ephesians 5:15-17 for encouragement to take good care of ourselves.

Weekly Readings Recap

Review the key themes of the week:

Day 1: The answer to our fragmented emotions, thoughts, and behaviors is standing firm in our identities in Christ, rather than allowing others to determine our identities. We can bring the things that others have said and done to us to God so that we can find healing and be made whole—integrated inside and out.

Day 2: When we are suffering on the inside, we don't want to think about beauty. To find healing and peace, we must reach out to Jesus. Peace is an inward calm that flows out through our facial expressions, attitudes, and behaviors. Even when our solutions seem limited or our circumstances seem hopeless, peace can get us through to the other side.

Day 3: The scars on our bodies tell many stories; we proudly show some scars while hiding others. Our scars are a constant reminder of certain life experiences that will never be erased from our memories or our bodies. When we consider the pain and difficulties that we face in this world, scars are a bittersweet yet appropriate metaphor for how God takes the horrible, painful events of our lives and redeems them.

Day 4: As followers of Christ, we are called to live a life of love—a beautiful representation of Christ's fragrant sacrifice for us. We are to share the inner beauty that comes from Christ with the world.

Day 5: Caring for ourselves and caring for others are not mutually exclusive. We don't have to abandon our obligations or those we love in order to take care of ourselves. And we don't have to feel guilty about it either. When we struggle to find the motivation to care for ourselves, we need to rely on God's wisdom and become obedient to that.

What You Will Need

- iPod or MP3 player with speakers or CD player and CD (see Preparing Your Hearts and Minds; optional song suggestion: Mandisa's "That's What Scars Are For")
- *Beautiful Already* DVD and DVD player
- stick-on name tags and markers
- index cards and pens

Session Objective

Today you will help the women in your group discover that beauty flows out of us toward others when we experience Jesus' peace and healing.

Session Outline

Preparing Your Hearts and Minds (2 minutes)

To help the women disconnect from the outside world and center their hearts on God, play a quiet, meaningful song as the women are gathering (optional song suggestion: Mandisa's "That's What Scars Are For"). When you are ready to begin the session, pray the opening prayer below or a prayer of your own.

Dear God, we want to win this ugly struggle with beauty. We know that You made us good and beautiful because You are good and beautiful. Reveal Your beauty in us and bring healing as we study Your word today. Amen.

Getting to Know Each Other (3–5 minutes)

Hand out the name tags and markers, and ask participants to write their names and wear the name tags for the session. Then, ask each woman to find a partner. Ask the pairs to discuss the following questions:

- What is your favorite thing about being a woman?
- What is your least favorite thing about being a woman?

After a couple of minutes, come back together as a full group and invite a few volunteers to share responses.

Video (25–30 minutes)

Play the Week 5 video segment on the DVD. Invite participants to complete the Video Viewer Guide for Week 5 in the participant book as they watch (page 161).

Group Discussion (20–25 minutes)

Video Discussion Questions

- Why is it often a struggle for us to take care of ourselves? What frees us from the guilt of taking care of ourselves?
- Why is self-care critical if we are to win the ugly struggle with beauty?
- What stood out or resonated most for you from the video teaching?

Participant Book Discussion Questions

More discussion points and questions have been provided than you will have time to include. Before the session, select those you want to cover, and put a check mark beside them. Page references are provided for questions related to questions or activities in the participant book. For these questions, invite participants to share the answers they wrote in their books.

1. While we as Christians understand that our identities are in Christ, we live in a society that doesn't share that belief; and there is confusion about what to believe regarding who we are as men and women. Jesus' willingness to come to earth as a man affirms the importance of our bodies and the integrated nature of our hearts, souls, minds, and bodies. (Day 1)
   - Read Galatians 2:20. How does Paul define his identity? (page 136)
   - If Christ lives within you as your identity, then what is the purpose of your life? (page 136)
   - When you are confused about your personal liberties or boundaries, whose standard will you rely upon? (page 136)

2. The danger of not knowing our identities in Christ is that we become fragmented in our emotions, thoughts, and behaviors without anything to unify us within ourselves. Such internal brokenness is profoundly painful. When we're fragmented, our fragmented choices lead to frustrating and fearful consequences. (Day 1)
   - When have you felt fragmented in your emotions, thoughts, or behaviors?
   - Have you ever had an identity crisis? If so, describe that time.
   - How does knowing that our identity is in Christ ground us when we feel unsure of who we are?

3. None of us escapes this life without wounds. Some of us have been hurt so deeply that we feel as if we are hemorrhaging our lifeblood, with no end in sight. (Day 2)
   - Read Mark 5:24-29. What do you learn about the woman and her condition? Why did the woman approach Jesus? What happened as soon as she touched his robe? (pages 139–140)
   - Is there something you've been suffering through for many years that has been draining your joy and energy for life? (page 140) How can this group support and encourage you?
   - Read Hebrews 4:15-16. What happens when we reach out to Jesus? (page 141) When have you reached out to Jesus and experienced His mercy?

4. Peace is living free from strife or worry. Peace is an inward calm that flows out through our facial expressions, attitudes, and behaviors. Even when our solutions seem limited or our circumstances seem hopeless, peace can get us through to the other side. (Day 2)
   - When have you known peace that got you through to the other side of a struggle? What was that like?
   - How can you share peace with others who might be suffering?
   - What did you learn about the meaning of the word *shalom* on Day 2? (See page 142.) How do we gain this type of deep peace?

5. The scars on our bodies tell many stories. Depending on what we've been through, we proudly show some scars while hiding others. Our scars are a constant reminder of certain life experiences that will never be erased from our memories or our bodies. Yet scars are an appropriate metaphor for how God takes the horrible, painful events of our lives and redeems them. When Jesus appeared to the disciples after the Resurrection, He invited them to look at His scars. He didn't hide that part of his story; those scars were a triumphant reminder of victory. (Day 3)
   - Where are some of your physical scars located? What are some of the stories behind your scars? (page 144)
   - How are scars a symbol of healing?
   - What do Jesus' scars mean for us? (page 144)

6. Some of our wounds are physical and evident, while others are emotional, relational, or spiritual and hidden deep inside. Here's the thing: our wounds will heal according to how healthy we are. If your wounds are related to your beauty narrative, then those wounds will heal only to the extent that you've uncovered the details of your beauty narrative. If your wounds are shame-based, those wounds won't heal unless you deal with shame. If your wounds remain open because of unforgiveness, they won't heal until you forgive. (Day 3)
   - Are your wounds healing well and forming appropriate scars? How do you know?
   - Review your victory story related to one aspect of your ugly struggle with beauty (pages 146–147). How would you summarize your struggle? What truth from God's Word brought healing? How can you encourage other women with your story?

7. As followers of Christ, we are called to live a life a love—a beautiful representation of Christ's fragrant sacrifice for us. (Day 4)
   - Read Ephesians 5:2. What is Jesus' sacrifice for us described as? How was Christ's sacrifice pleasing to God? How does the Apostle Paul call us to follow Christ's example? (page 151)

- Read Mark 14:1-9. What type of container did the woman bring into the house with her, and what was in that container? What did she do with the perfume? Why was she criticized by those around the table? What was Jesus' response to her critics? (page 152)
- What would it mean for you to be a "Christlike fragrance rising up to God" each day? What are some clues that might indicate your life is giving off a Christlike fragrance? (page 152)

8. As long as there is someone else in our lives to care for, we often are tempted to put ourselves at the back of the line. Caring for ourselves and caring for others are not mutually exclusive. We don't have to abandon our obligations or those we love in order to take care of ourselves. And we don't have to feel guilty about it either. (Day 5)
   - Which season describes your life right now? What impact is this season of life having on your desire or ability to care for yourself—internally and externally? (page 156)
   - Why do you think we women struggle so much with self-care? Why do you think we're often reluctant to do something nice for ourselves?
   - When have you been intentional about a self-care indulgence? What did that feel like?
   - What are some potential spiritual consequences that might arise from our lack of physical self-care? (page 158)

9. In 1 Corinthians 6, the Apostle Paul challenges us with the realization that our bodies do not belong to ourselves but to God. When we're in a busy or difficult season, we tend to look out for everyone around us, and we are the ones we stop looking out for. Yet God doesn't want worry to warp our perspective. (Day 5)
   - Read 1 Corinthians 6:19-20. What is the price that God paid for our bodies? What are the things we need to do in order to honor God with our bodies? What are some of the things you need to avoid in order to honor God? (page 157)
   - Read 1 Peter 5:7. What should we do with our worries and cares? How hard is it for you to give your worries over to God? What happens to our hearts and minds when we give our worries to God instead of carrying them around? (pages 157–158)

10. Wrap up group discussion with these questions:
    - What is something that surprised you in your study this week?
    - What did you learn this week about God? About yourself?
    - How does it impact your life to realize that Jesus can heal our wounds and restore us, creating an inner beauty that radiates outward?

*Live It Out (10 minutes)

If you are meeting for 90 minutes, ask everyone to turn to a neighbor and talk about one or more **Live It Out** reflections from the weekly readings. If possible, try to come back together for the last few minutes of this segment and invite a few volunteers to share some highlights from their conversations.

*Group Activity (15 minutes)

Hand out index cards and pens. Ask participants to make themselves coupons for self-care. Invite them to think of one act of self-care they'll give themselves permission to do, using this coupon as a reminder. This could be going to get a manicure, buying a book online, going for coffee with a friend, and so on. When they are finished, ask some volunteers to share their coupon with the group.

Closing Prayer (3 minutes)

Close the session by taking personal prayer requests from group members and leading the group in prayer. Encourage members to participate in the closing prayer by praying out loud for one another and the requests given. Remind group members to pray for one another throughout the week.

Week 6

DISCOVERING YOUR BEAUTY BALANCE

Leader Prep

Scripture and Theme Overview

This week's theme is about finding our beauty balance, which gives us freedom to live and love. We discovered that both inner and outer beauty have their place as long as we cultivate them in the right balance, and we saw that this balance is a matter of proportion, not equality. We learned what it means to be a woman who CARES. by exploring five aspects of outer beauty (Clothes/appearance, Appetite, Rest, Exercise, Smile). We began by looking at Scriptures about modesty and making good choices (Proverbs 11:22; 31:30; 1 Timothy 2:9-10). Then we looked to the story of Jacob and Esau in Genesis 25 to understand how hunger and appetite can be dangerous, as well as the story of Jesus' temptation in Matthew 4 to find the solution for our deepest hungers (Matthew 4). We returned to the creation story to see why and how God created the Sabbath (Genesis 2:2-3), and we explored the importance of taking a regular Sabbath rest. Next we mined various Scriptures that point to the value of developing strong, fit bodies as well as the impact that happiness and gratitude have in our lives. Finally, we looked again to the story of Esther to see a shining example of the balance of physical and inner beauty.

Weekly Readings Recap

Review the key themes of the week:

Day 1: When we dress with dignity, we dress in a way that causes people to honor and respect us for how we appear to them. This is not the kind of honor and respect that elevates us above others but the kind that reflects who God created us to be.

Day 2: If left unchecked, your appetite can control your relationship with food. But when you are aware of your physical and emotional condition, then you can remind yourself that food won't fill that deep void; only dependence on God will.

Day 3: Sabbath is about learning how to "be" and breaking away from the rhythm of "doing." It's a spiritual principle that calls us to learn how to trust in God instead of believing that everything depends on our own efforts.

Day 4: Doing whatever we can do to take care of our bodies helps each of us to give all that we can for God's purposes in our lives and our world. Even when we are limited physically, we can use our bodies to the best of our ability for the glory of God.

Day 5: If we put all of our effort into pursuing physical beauty, we aren't going to have what it takes when the pressure builds up in our lives. Inner beauty gives us the courage to walk with conviction instead of giving ourselves over to what feels right in the moment or reacting out of fear. Inner beauty explains the decision to display kindness rather than anger or the decision to display humility when snarkiness or disrespectfulness might feel better in the moment.

What You Will Need

- iPod or MP3 player with speakers or CD player and CD (see Preparing Your Hearts and Minds and the Group Activity)
- *Beautiful Already* DVD and DVD player
- stick-on name tags and markers
- the song "The Broken Beautiful" by Ellie Holcomb

Session Objective

Today you will help the women in your group end this study with confidence in their God-given beauty and their ability to find the right balance or proportion between inner and outer beauty.

Session Outline

Preparing Your Hearts and Minds (2 minutes)

To help the women disconnect from the outside world and center their hearts on God, play a quiet, meaningful song as the women are gathering. When you are ready to begin the session, pray the opening prayer below or a prayer of your own.

Dear God, thank You for this time we've had together exploring beauty. Help us to look in the mirror with all the confidence of daughters of God. Bless us with Your love and wisdom as we talk about what it means to find the right balance between inner and outer beauty, and prepare us to walk out the truths we've learned in this study. In Jesus' name we pray. Amen.

Getting to Know Each Other (3–5 minutes)

Hand out the name tags and markers, and ask participants to write their names and wear the name tags for the session. Then, ask each woman to find a partner. Ask the pairs to discuss the following questions:

- When you fall into emotional eating, what is your must-have food item?
- What is your favorite kind of workout?

After a couple of minutes, come back together as a full group and invite the women to share a few responses.

Video (25-30 minutes)

Play the Week 6 video segment on the DVD. Invite participants to complete the Video Viewer Guide for Week 6 in the participant book as they watch (pages 196–197).

Group Discussion (20–25 minutes)

Video Discussion Questions

- Why is balancing inner and outer beauty not a 50/50 proposition? How does it help you to know that the proportion is going to be unique for each of us?

- What insights have you gained about what it means to be a beautiful woman on the inside and out?
- What stood out or resonated most for you from the video teaching?

Participant Book Discussion Questions

More discussion points and questions have been provided than you will have time to include. Before the session, select those you want to cover, and put a check mark beside them. Page references are provided for questions related to questions or activities in the participant book. For these questions, invite participants to share the answers they wrote in their books.

1. If God judges the heart, is clothing a spiritual topic, then? In a sense, yes. Because our bodies are created by God and we are called by God to be holy in all that we say and do, this means there is a spiritual element to the clothing that we wear. Furthermore, it's up to us to understand how the clothes we wear are a reflection of our ABCs: attitude, beliefs, and character. (Day 1)
   - Do you think there is a spiritual element to our clothing choices? Why or why not?
   - How are clothes a reflection of our attitudes, beliefs, and character?
   - What are the three questions we need to ask ourselves about our clothes?
   - What is your general attitude about clothes? What are some words you would use to describe the clothes in your closet? (page 166)
   - What are some of your favorite items of clothing?

2. One of the keys to knowing what to buy and wear is knowing who you are in Christ. Your identity as a beautiful woman rooted in Christ serves as a helpful filter when you shop and get dressed. When we possess sensitivity, we recognize that although we are in control of what we wear, our choices have an impact on others. When we dress with dignity, we dress in a way that causes people to honor and respect us for how we appear to them. This is not the kind of honor and respect that elevates us above others but the kind that reflects who God created us to be. (Day 1)
   - Read 1 Corinthians 10:23. How does this verse apply to our clothing choices? What kind of tension is created when we dress in a manner that is contrary to our faith? (page 167)
   - What are some of your personal boundaries when it comes to dressing? What are some things that you refrain from wearing because it could be offensive or distracting to others? (page 167)
   - How would you explain the difference between dressing attractively and dressing sensually or seductively? (page 169)

- Read Proverbs 31:30. What is given the greatest value in this verse? (page 170) Why is the fear of the Lord greater than beauty?

3. The fact that we have appetites is neither bad nor good; however, everything rides on how we will satisfy those appetites when they arise. How you manage your desire for love, acceptance, achievement, and connection determines whether you are controlling your appetite or your appetite is controlling you. (Day 2)
   - Have you ever experienced a time when your appetite controlled you? Describe that time.
   - Why is an appetite neither bad nor good?
   - Why is it important to know the difference between needing something and desiring something?

4. The story of Jacob and Esau in the Old Testament teaches us about the danger of appetite. Though it is tempting to judge Esau for such a rash, foolish decision, we've all experienced something similar. We women are notorious emotional eaters. When our hunger for stability, healing, peace, acceptance, or love goes unsatisfied, we often seek satisfaction in food. (Day 2)
   - Read Genesis 25:31-34. What did Jacob ask for in return for giving Esau food? Why do you think Esau would trade the birthright—something so valuable—for a bowl of stew, which was only temporary? (page 173)
   - What kinds of foods do you pick up and have difficulty putting down when you are hurting? (page 174)
   - Read Matthew 4:1-4. How long did Jesus go without food? What did Satan suggest to Jesus? What was Jesus' response to Satan? (page 174)
   - What did you learn about how to manage your appetite and handle the urge to eat emotionally? As you consider these ways to manage your appetite, what are some action steps you need to consider taking in your life? (page 176)

5. Friends, burnout is not beautiful. Neither are bags under our eyes or nerves that are frayed because we've been stretched far beyond what's reasonable. We must take time to rest. We see the importance of rest from the very beginning. (Day 3)
   - When have you known extreme fatigue or burnout?
   - Read Genesis 2:2-3. What does this verse tell us about the seventh day? How did God define or describe that day of rest? (page 179)
   - Why is it important to understand that God rested, not because He was tired, but because He was pleased?

6. One of the key principles behind the Sabbath is trusting God to be God while we care for our bodies. Friends, we can run that errand or return that e-mail, but taking care of that "one" thing will cost us the blessing that God wants to give us: rest. Rest blesses us. (Day 3)
   - What are three ways that rest blesses us?
   - If you struggle to take a Sabbath rest, what are some of the barriers that prevent you from ceasing your regular work (including errands) one day a week? (page 180)
   - Read Mark 2:27. What did Jesus mean by this? (page 181)
   - Where and how will you add a time of Sabbath into your week?
   - What are your favorite ways to reconnect with God? (page 182)

7. As Christian women, we have the best reason of all to be healthy and fit: the gospel! Even though I don't love to exercise, that's my reason for staying fit—so I can give my all to sharing the message of God's love and serving others in the name of Jesus Christ. (Day 4)
   - How can staying fit help us share the gospel?
   - Read 1 Corinthians 6:19-20. How is our body described? How does caring for our physical bodies honor God? (page 187)
   - Why do you think only roughly 50 percent of women exercise? Do you agree that many women are afraid of what people will think of them while they exercise? Why or why not?
   - What are your fitness goals right now? How can you invite others to support you in those goals?

8. Smiling has both physical and emotional effects that can change our attitude and outlook. Yet despite both physiological and scriptural reasons for smiling, at times we can find it difficult to smile. (Day 4)
   - Would you say that you are a person who smiles easily or naturally? Why or why not? What makes you smile most often?
   - In those times when you've found yourself struggling to smile, what have been some of the common reasons for your struggle? (page 189)
   - Read Proverbs 15:13; Proverbs 15:30; Proverbs 17:22. What do these verses tell us about the impact that happiness and gratitude have in our lives? (page 189)
   - How can a simple smile from you be a blessing to others? How might it help to spread the gospel?

9. If we put all of our effort into pursuing physical beauty, we aren't going to have what it takes when the pressure builds up in our lives. When tragedy strikes or when relationships run off course, long eyelashes and the perfect outfit don't mean a thing. Inner beauty gives us the courage to walk with

conviction instead of giving ourselves over to what feels right in the moment or reacting out of fear. Inner beauty explains the decision to display kindness rather than anger or the decision to display humility when snarkiness or disrespectfulness might feel better in the moment. (Day 5)

- Review Esther 2. How do we know that Esther possessed physical beauty?
- Read Esther 2:15. How did Esther demonstrate gentleness (humility) and wisdom? (page 192)
- Read Esther 4:1-17. What was the question that Mordecai asked Esther? (page 193) How did both Esther's inner beauty and physical beauty play a part in saving her people?

10. While Esther displayed qualities that we'd associate with a gentle and quiet spirit, she also had to fight through fear and demonstrate courage because the lives of the entire Jewish race were at risk. Esther shows us that strength and beauty complement each other perfectly. (Day 5)

- When have you needed both strength and beauty to get through a hard season in your life?
- In what ways is Esther a great role model for us in our ugly struggle with beauty?
- How could accepting your God-given beauty, seeking God first in all things, and boldly claiming your identity as a beloved and beautiful masterpiece of the Creator of the universe make you uniquely ready when a "such a time as this" moment comes in your life?

11. Wrap up group discussion with these questions:

- What is something that surprised you in your study this week?
- What did you learn this week about God? About yourself?
- How does it impact your life to realize that physical and inner beauty work together to help you point others to God?
- What is your biggest takeaway from this study?
- How will your life be different because of the time you have spent studying the Bible and sharing with the women gathered here?

*Live It Out (10 minutes)

If you are meeting for 90 minutes, ask everyone to turn to a neighbor and talk about one or more **Live It Out** reflections from the weekly readings. If possible, try to come back together for the last few minutes of this segment and invite a few volunteers to share some highlights from their conversations.

*Group Activity (15 minutes)

Invite participants into a time of worship to close your study. Play the song "The Broken Beautiful" by Ellie Holcomb. Ask the women to listen prayerfully and let the promise that God makes broken things beautiful wash over them. Then lead the following prayer, inviting participants to respond with the phrase "We are Beautiful Already" whenever you pause. (You might indicate it is their turn by extending a hand.)

Leader: God, when we look in the mirror and see only our faults…

All: We are beautiful already.

Leader: When we've tried on every outfit and nothing makes us feel pretty…

All: We are beautiful already.

Leader: When our scars remind us of the pain instead of the healing…

All: We are beautiful already.

Leader: When we are stuck in our attempts at fitness and healthy eating…

All: We are beautiful already.

Leader: When we forget who we are and to whom we belong…

All: We are beautiful already.

Leader: God, help us to see ourselves the way You see us. Help us to seek You first in everything—even in our quest to grow in physical and inner beauty. Remind us that You made us and that we are Your masterpieces. Speak Your words of beauty and grace and acceptance into the deepest, darkest corners of our hearts and minds. Overcome our ugly narratives with your beautiful words. God, we love You. You are beautiful. Thank You for being so very good to us. In Jesus' name, we pray. Amen.

Closing Prayer (3 minutes)

Close your time together by extending hugs and words of affirmation to one another. Encourage participants to continue praying for one another and to stay in touch as they are able in the weeks to come.

Group Roster

	Name	Phone Number	E-mail
1.			
2.			
3.			
4.			
5.			
6.			
7.			
8.			
9.			
10.			
11.			
12.			
13.			
14.			
15.			
16.			
17.			
18.			
19.			
20.			
21.			
22.			
23.			
24.			
25.			

Meet Our Abingdon Women Authors

Jessica LaGrone is Dean of the Chapel at Asbury Theological Seminary and an acclaimed pastor, teacher, and speaker who enjoys leading retreats and events throughout the United States. She previously served as Pastor of Creative Ministries at The Woodlands UMC in Houston, Texas. She is the author of *Namesake: When God Rewrites Your Story*, *Broken and Blessed: How God Changed the World Through One Imperfect Family*, and *Set Apart: Holy Habits of Prophets and Kings*. She and her husband, Jim, have two young children. For speaking and booking information and to follow her blog, Reverend Mother, visit JessicaLagrone.com.

Babbie Mason is an award-winning singer and songwriter; a women's conference speaker; a leader of worship celebration-concerts for women; adjunct professor of songwriting at Lee University; and television talk-show host of *Babbie's House*. She has led worship for national and international events hosted by Billy Graham, Charles Stanley, Anne Graham Lotz, Women of Faith, and others. She is the author of *Embraced by God* and *This I Know for Sure*. For information about speaking and events, visit Babbie.com.

Barbara L. Roose is a popular speaker and author who is passionate about connecting women to one another and to God. Previously Barb was Executive Director of Ministry at CedarCreek Church in Perrysburg, Ohio, where she served on staff for fourteen years and co-led the annual Fabulous Women's Conference. Barb is a frequent speaker at women's conferences and other events. She lives in Toledo, Ohio, with her husband, Matt. They are the proud parents of three beautiful daughters, two dogs, and a grumpy rabbit named Pal. For events and booking information and to follow her blog, visit BarbRoose.com.

Get more information at

Kimberly Dunnam Reisman is known for her effective and engaging preaching and teaching. Kim is the World Director of World Methodist Evangelism and has served as the Executive Director of Next Step Evangelism Ministries and Adjunct Professor at United Theological Seminary. Kim is the author or co-author of numerous books and studies, including *The Christ-Centered Woman: Finding Balance in a World of Extremes*. The mother of three adult children, Kim and her husband live in West Lafayette, Indiana. For information about speaking and events, visit KimberlyReisman.com.

Melissa Spoelstra is a popular women's conference speaker, Bible teacher, and writer who is passionate about helping other women to seek Christ and know Him more intimately through serious Bible study. She is the author of the Bible studies *Jeremiah: Daring to Hope in an Unstable World*, *Joseph: The Journey to Forgiveness*, and *First Corinthians: Living Love When We Disagree* (August 2016). She is also the author of the forthcoming book, *Total Family Makeover*. She lives in Dublin, Ohio, with her pastor husband and four kids. For events and booking information and to follow her blog, visit MelissaSpoelstra.com.

Cindi Wood is a sought-after speaker and Bible teacher with events throughout the United States and abroad. Through biblically-based teaching coupled with humor from daily experience, Cindi offers hope and encouragement to women of all ages and walks of life. She is the author of numerous books and Bible studies, including *Anonymous: Discovering the Somebody You Are to God* and the Frazzled Female series. Cindi lives in Kings Mountain, North Carolina, with her husband, Larry. For events and booking information, visit FrazzledFemale.com.

AbingdonWomen.com.

CPSIA information can be obtained at www.ICGtesting.com
Printed in the USA
LVOW09s1110160616

492880LV00002B/3/P